JUMP INTO JOBS
TECHNOLOGY JOBS

Written by Kay Barnham

Illustrations by Jennifer Naalchigar

Enslow
PUBLISHING

Published in 2026 by Enslow Publishing, LLC
2544 Clinton Street
Buffalo, NY 14224

First published in Great Britain in 2025
by Wayland

Copyright © Hodder and Stoughton, 2025

Editor: Amy Pimperton
Designer: Lisa Peacock

Cataloging-in-Publication Data

Names: Barnham, Kay. | Naalchigar, Jennifer, illustrator.
Title: Technology jobs / Kay Barnham, illustrations by Jennifer Naalchigar.
Description: Buffalo, NY : Enslow Publishing, 2026. | Series: Jump into jobs | Includes glossary and index.
Identifiers: ISBN 9781978545748 (pbk.) | ISBN 9781978545755 (library bound) | ISBN 9781978545762 (ebook)
Subjects: LCSH: Technology--Vocational guidance--Juvenile literature.
Classification: LCC T65.3 B376 2026 | DDC 602.3--dc23

All rights reserved. No part of this book may be reproduced in any form without permission in writing from the publisher, except by a reviewer.

Manufactured in the United States of America

CPSIA compliance information: Batch #CSENS26: For further information contact Enslow Publishing LLC, New York, New York at 1-800-398-2504.

Please visit our website, www.enslowpublishing.com. For a free color catalog of all our high-quality books, call toll free 1-800-398-2504 or fax 1-877-980-4454.

Find us on

CONTENTS

Meet Billie ... and Mia!	4
Space suit designers ... help astronauts survive	6
Game designers ... create worlds	8
Computer programmers ... turn ideas into code	10
Robotics engineers ... control robots	12
Mechanical engineers ... make machines work	14
Biomedical engineers ... help doctors and patients	16
Transmission line engineers ... move electricity	18
Electricians ... make electricity work	20
Recycling technicians ... reuse and recycle	22
Web developers ... make online shine	24
E-bike designers ... power the pedals	26
Now it's your turn to work with technology!	28
Glossary	30
Further information	31
Index	32

MEET BILLIE ... AND MIA!

Here are some of the things that Billie likes best: Mia the cat, science, technology, and asking lots of questions like these ...

What is technology?

Is it easy to build a robot?

Who knows how machines work?

(Here are some of the things that Mia likes best: automatic cat flaps, sleeping in front of a warm heater, and Billie.)

Billie would like to work in technology, but doesn't know which career to choose. There are so many!

Luckily, Billie's dress-up box is the perfect place to start. It's bursting with great outfits! When they dress up, Billie and Mia are whisked away to meet the people who wear these clothes in real life ... and find out all about the jobs they do.

Let's go and meet the supersmart people who work in technology!

Billie chooses a calculator and a space suit.
These are perfect for a technology adventure.

5

SPACE SUIT DESIGNERS ... HELP ASTRONAUTS SURVIVE

SPACE SUIT DESIGNERS use their knowledge of textiles and technology to create clothing that keeps astronauts alive in space.

In space, there's no air, so space suits are designed to supply oxygen. And it can be very cold, but the sun's glare is very hot. Space suits have many special layers to keep astronauts at a safe, steady temperature.

This space suit provides drinking water too!

Space suits are tough to protect astronauts from space dust, which can travel at dangerously high speeds. But they are also flexible, so astronauts can move easily in them.

Who else uses technology to design things?

SPACE SUIT DESIGNERS:
- know all about textiles
- love a challenge
- are experts in chemistry and physics.

GAME DESIGNERS ... CREATE WORLDS

GAME DESIGNERS invent video games, so players can visit virtual worlds for amazing adventures.

My new character will go from planet to planet in search of jewels!

When they are creating a new product, game designers have many decisions to make. They must decide what type of game theirs will be, what the characters will look like and how the game will work. They also need to think up an exciting story!

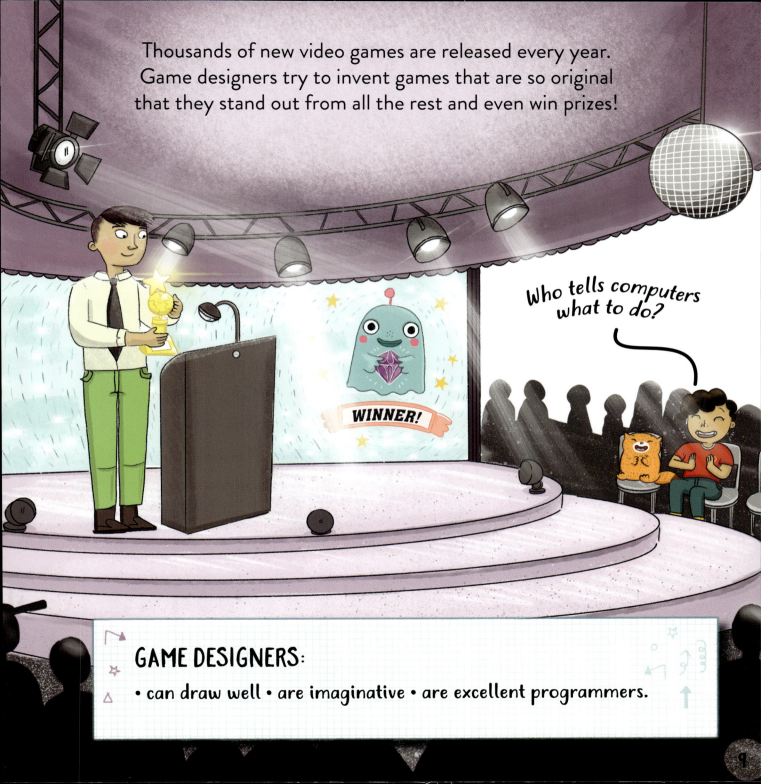

COMPUTER PROGRAMMERS...
TURN IDEAS INTO CODE

COMPUTER PROGRAMMERS tell computers how to do different jobs. They do this by writing instructions in code, which is a language that computers understand.

Computers can do many things. They can change the colors of traffic lights, work out complicated sums, and even send a rocket into space. But they can't do anything without a computer programmer telling them how to!

A computer programmer might write a huge amount of code to describe even the simplest task to a computer.

I'm writing code that will tell a computer how to open and close this bridge.

Who else uses computer code in their job?

COMPUTER PROGRAMMERS:
• are very logical • are excellent at math • are great at problem-solving.

ROBOTICS ENGINEERS...
CONTROL ROBOTS

Some jobs can be dull, repetitive, or dangerous. **ROBOTICS ENGINEERS** build robots that can do these jobs so humans don't have to!

Robotics engineers design robots, build them, repair them, and write computer programs that make the robots work.

I'm programming these robots to spray cars with paint and not waste a single drop!

MECHANICAL ENGINEERS ... MAKE MACHINES WORK

When a job needs to be done, **MECHANICAL ENGINEERS** find the best way to do it. Then they create a machine or device that will do that job.

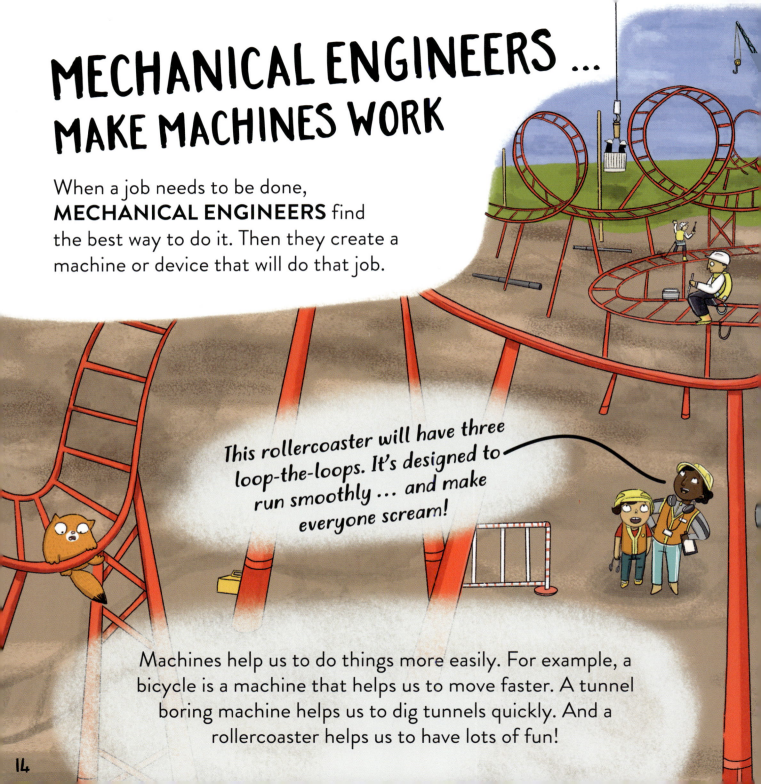

This rollercoaster will have three loop-the-loops. It's designed to run smoothly ... and make everyone scream!

Machines help us to do things more easily. For example, a bicycle is a machine that helps us to move faster. A tunnel boring machine helps us to dig tunnels quickly. And a rollercoaster helps us to have lots of fun!

But mechanical engineers don't just design and build machines. When machines go wrong, they figure out ways to fix them too. They love to find solutions to problems!

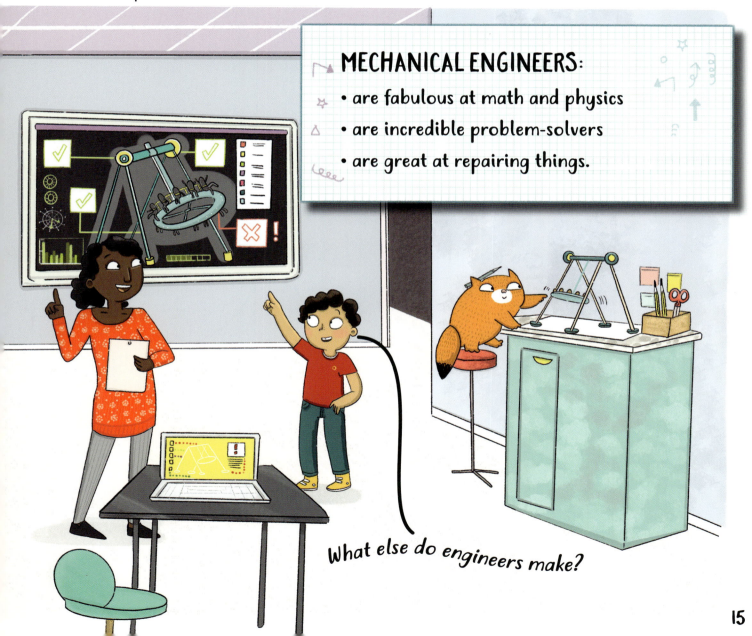

MECHANICAL ENGINEERS:
- are fabulous at math and physics
- are incredible problem-solvers
- are great at repairing things.

What else do engineers make?

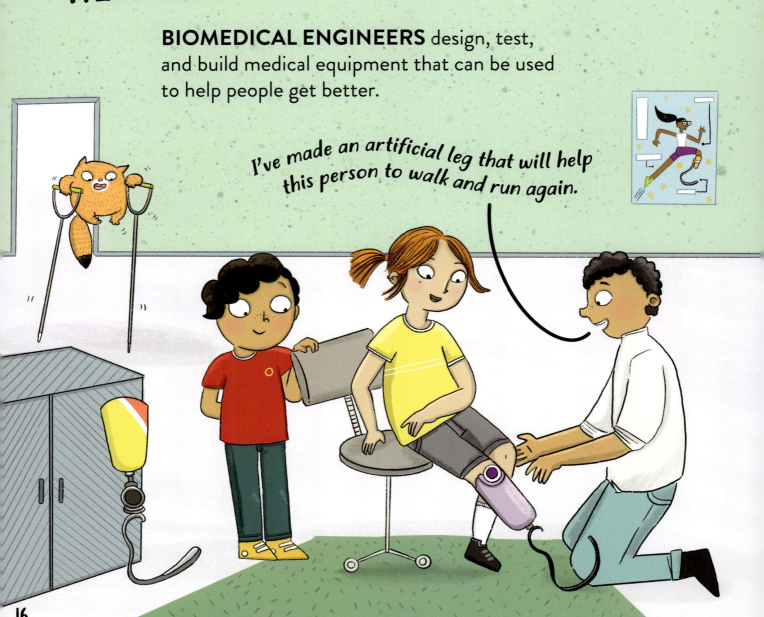

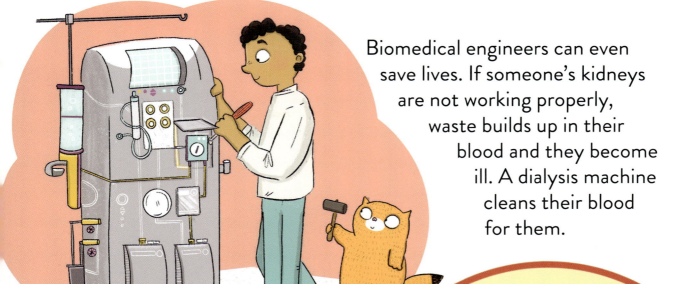

Biomedical engineers can even save lives. If someone's kidneys are not working properly, waste builds up in their blood and they become ill. A dialysis machine cleans their blood for them.

In every hospital, you'll find machines built by biomedical engineers. Some X-ray people's bodies to see if there are broken bones. Others monitor heartbeats.

What powers machines like this heartbeat monitor?

BIOMEDICAL ENGINEERS:
• know how the human body works • are inventive • are marvelous at math.

17

TRANSMISSION LINE ENGINEERS ... MOVE ELECTRICITY

Electricity is a type of energy that we use every day to make things such as fridges and computers work. **TRANSMISSION LINE ENGINEERS** make sure that electricity can travel safely to wherever it is needed!

Our helicopter team checks electricity transmission towers and power lines from the sky. If anything's broken, we'll fix it!

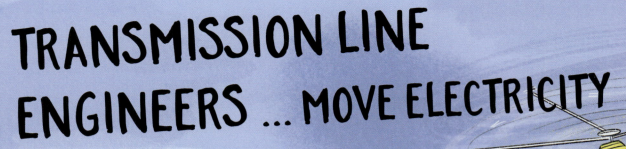

TRANSMISSION LINE ENGINEERS:
- work well in a team • are great at physics
- are used to working on VERY BIG projects.

ELECTRICIANS ... MAKE ELECTRICITY WORK

When electricity reaches homes, schools, offices, and factories, it's an **ELECTRICIAN**'s job to deal with it. They make sure everything electrical works properly and safely!

It's very important to turn off the electricity supply before I start work. Electricity gives a VERY big shock!

Even small amounts of electricity can be dangerous. So, only qualified electricians should fix electrical systems and make sure they are safe. Electricians set up lights, sockets, and switches too.

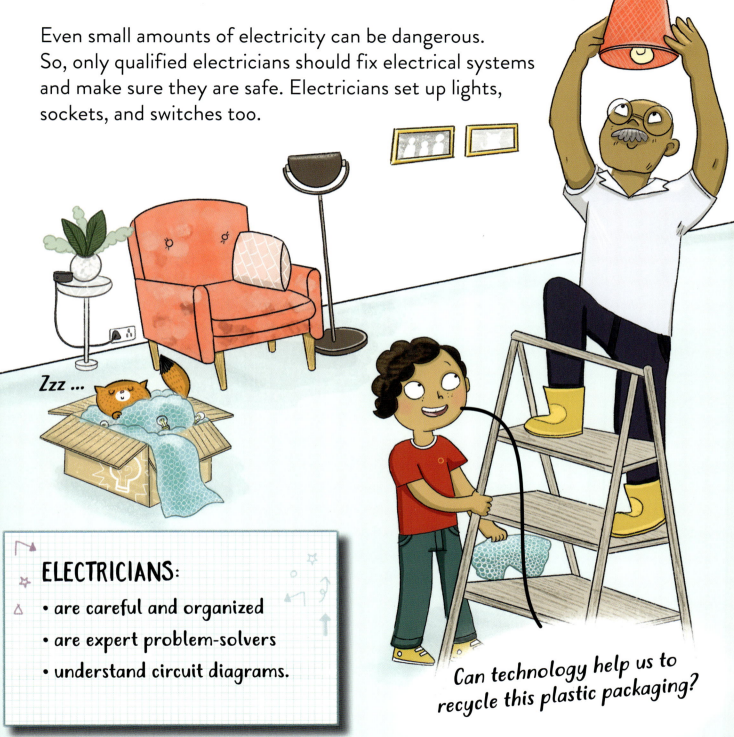

Zzz ...

ELECTRICIANS:
- are careful and organized
- are expert problem-solvers
- understand circuit diagrams.

Can technology help us to recycle this plastic packaging?

RECYCLING TECHNICIANS ... REUSE AND RECYCLE

RECYCLING TECHNICIANS deal with cardboard, plastic, metal, and glass waste from homes and businesses. They help to process them into new materials.

Recycling technicians also deal with large pieces of technology, such as wind turbines, which turn wind energy into electricity.

At the end of their life, recycling technicians take the wind turbines apart. Then they recycle the concrete, steel, copper, aluminium, and plastics used to make them.

Most of this wind turbine can be recycled or reused!

Fiberglass turbine blades are hard to recycle, so they are reused instead. They have been used to build parks, bridges, and bike shelters!

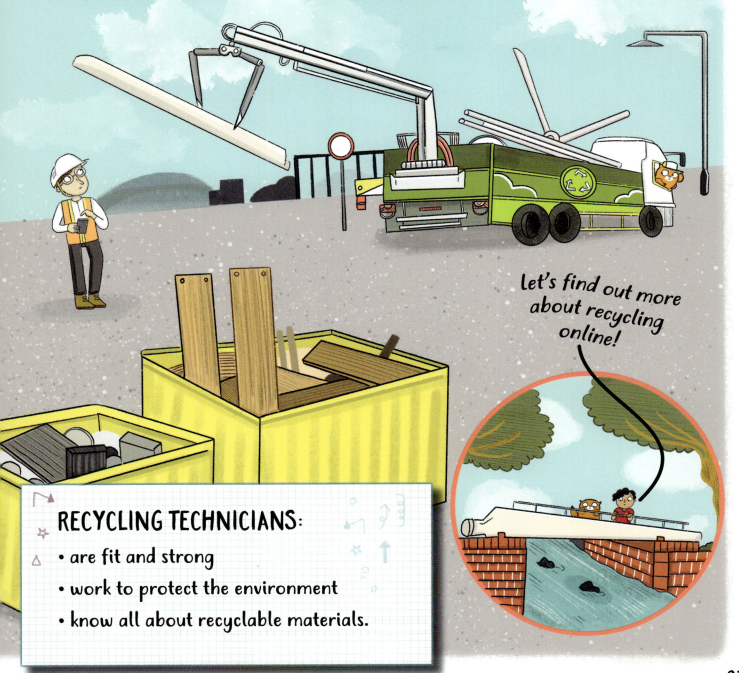

let's find out more about recycling online!

RECYCLING TECHNICIANS:
- are fit and strong
- work to protect the environment
- know all about recyclable materials.

WEB DEVELOPERS... MAKE ONLINE SHINE

The internet is bursting with information. **WEB DEVELOPERS** create websites that are easy to understand and use.

My job is to check that this website works properly before it goes live tomorrow!

If websites were just filled with tiny words, they would be very dull. So, web developers use color, pictures, videos, and words of different sizes instead. This helps them to design websites that look great!

Web developers write code so websites are simple to use – this make it easy for us to click around online. They also update websites when information changes.

Who makes cool e-bikes like this?

WEB DEVELOPERS:
- are computer code experts
- are great designers • work well with others.

25

E-BIKE DESIGNERS...
POWER THE PEDALS

E-BIKE DESIGNERS create bikes that use battery power to speed along. It's their job to design machines that help cyclists to go faster and further!

E-bike designers develop bikes that are sturdy enough to carry a battery and an electric motor, but sleek enough to speed along. They also need to look super cool so cyclists will want to ride them!

E-mountain bikes are very tough with bouncy suspension, so that they can be used on bumpy ground.

Our technology adventure was fun, but tiring. It's time to *pedal home!*

E-BIKE DESIGNERS:
- understand computer design
- are fabulous at physics
- love mechanical and electrical engineering.

NOW IT'S YOUR TURN TO WORK WITH TECHNOLOGY!

Like Billie and Mia, do you love the idea of working with technology? Do you enjoy finding out how things work? Do you like solving problems? If this sounds like you, then here are some ideas for what to do next.

1. Invent your own video game. What do players need to do to win? Which special powers and tools can they use? Try to come up with an idea that no one else has thought of. Don't forget to give it a cool name!

2. Become a recycling-plant technician for a day by sorting out all of the recycling at home. Ask an adult to help you to split it into different piles to figure out which material is recycled most. What could this be turned into?

3. Build a robot from a cardboard box! Add knobs, levers, windows, foil, and anything else you can think of to make it look like the real thing. When you're finished, write a manual to show users how your robot works and what it does!

GLOSSARY

artificial something that has been made by humans

automatic when a machine does something by itself

character someone in a story, a film or a computer game

circuit diagram a drawing that shows how electricity flows inside a machine or around a building

complicated difficult

computer code instructions written for a computer

dialysis a way of cleaning blood

environment the world around us

fiberglass a tough material made of glass strands and plastic

logical someone who makes clear and sensible decisions

oxygen a gas we breathe to survive

practical someone who is very good at getting things done

qualified someone who has been trained and passed a test to do a job

space dust dust in space that comes from comets and asteroids

suspension a system for a bike that cushions bumps so the cyclist has a smoother ride

textiles different materials, such as cotton, nylon, silk, and wool

transmission tower a tall metal tower used to carry electricity cables high in the air

website a collection of pages on the internet where people can find out information

X-rays waves of energy that can be used to photograph our insides and show when bones are broken, for example

FURTHER INFORMATION

BOOKS TO READ

Allen, John. *Exploring Careers in AI*. San Diego, CA: ReferencePoint Press, Inc., 2025.

Hubbard, Ben. *Adventures in Technology*. Buffalo, NY: Enslow Publishing, 2026.

Morkes, Andrew. *Space: Scientists and Engineers*. Hollywood, FL: Mason Crest, 2024.

WEBSITES TO VISIT

The Science Museum website has a section on the stories behind everyday technology items.
www.sciencemuseum.org.uk/objects-and-stories/everyday-technology

The Jam Coding website has advice for parents and children about interesting career paths in technology.
https://jamcoding.co.uk/8-jobs-your-child-can-do-with-the-right-digital-skills/

The website addresses (URLs) in this book were valid at the time of going to press. However, it is possible that the contents or addresses may have changed since the publication of this book. No responsibility for any such changes can be accepted by either the author or the Publisher. We strongly advise that internet access is supervised by a responsible adult.

INDEX

astronauts 6–7

batteries 26

computer code 10–11, 25
computer games 8–9, 29
computer programmers 9, 10–11, 12
computers 8–11, 18, 27

designers 6–7, 8, 12, 15, 16, 19, 25

e-bikes 25, 26–27
electricians 20–21
electricity 18–21, 26
engineers 15
   biomedical 16–17
   electrical 18–19, 27

mechanical 14–15, 27
robotics 12–13
transmission line 18–19

internet 23, 24

logic 11, 13

machines 13, 14–15, 17, 26
   repairing 15, 17
materials 22–23, 29
math 11, 13, 15, 17
medicine 16–17

recycling 21, 22–23, 29
robots 12–13, 29

science 4, 7, 13, 15, 18, 27

space 6–7, 10
space suits 5, 6–7

web developers 24–25
websites 24–25